THE LIFE AND MUSIC OF PHIL LESH

Let's talk about the life of a member and bassist for an iconic rock band grateful dead

A Deep Dive into the Life of a Rock and Roll Icon, from the Early Days to the Grateful Dead and Beyond

Norman Osaro

Copyright © 2024 by Norman Osaro

All rights reserved. No part of this publication may be reproduced, distributed, or transmitted in any form or by any means, including photocopying, recording, or other electronic or mechanical methods, without the prior written permission of the publisher, except in the case of brief quotations embodied in critical reviews and certain other noncommercial uses permitted by copyright law.

Table of content

INTRODUCTION

CHAPTER 1: EARLY LIFE AND MUSICAL BEGINNERS
- ★ A Classical Foundation
- ★ Discovering the Bass Guitar

CHAPTER 2: THE BIRTH OF THE GRATEFUL DEAD
- ★ A Psychedelic Journey
- ★ Shaping the Sound of a Generation

CHAPTER 3 : A MUSICAL MAESTRO
- ★ The Heartbeat of the Band
- ★ Innovative Bass Playing and Improvisation

CHAPTER 4: BEYOND THE GRATEFUL DEAD
- ★ Solo Projects and Collaborations

★ Terrapin Crossroads: A Gathering Place for Music Lovers

CHAPTER 5: LEGACY AND IMPACT
 ★ Inspiring Generations of Musicians
 ★ Is Enduring Spirit

Conclusion

INTRODUCTION

Phil Lesh, the enigmatic bassist of the Grateful Dead, was more than just a musician. He was a sonic architect, a visionary who shaped the sound of a generation. His deep, resonant bass lines provided the rhythmic heartbeat of the band, driving their improvisational journeys into the stratosphere.

This biography is a deep dive into the life of a rock and roll icon, from his early days as a classical musician to his legendary tenure with the Grateful Dead and beyond. We'll explore his musical genius, his unwavering dedication to his craft, and his enduring impact on the world of music.

Prepare to be transported back to the psychedelic era, to feel the power of live music, and to understand the profound influence of Phil Lesh. As you turn the pages of this book, you'll discover the man behind the music, the innovator, the inspiration, and the legend.

CHAPTER 1: EARLY LIFE AND MUSICAL BEGINNERS

A Classical Foundation

Phil Lesh, the man who would become the heartbeat of the Grateful Dead, was born on March 15, 1940, in Berkeley, California. His early life was marked by a deep love for music, a passion that would shape his future.

Lesh's musical journey began with classical training. As a young boy, he immersed himself in the world of classical music, learning to play the cello. This classical foundation would prove to be invaluable as he later transitioned to the electric bass guitar. The discipline and technical proficiency he gained from classical training would serve him well throughout his career.

However, it was the electric bass guitar that truly captured Lesh's heart. Drawn to the instrument's versatility and its ability to drive a band's rhythm section, he began exploring the world of rock and roll. He was captivated by the energy and innovation of musicians like Chuck Berry and

Little Richard, and he yearned to be a part of the music scene.

As Lesh delved deeper into the world of rock and roll, he began to develop his own unique style of playing. He was influenced by a wide range of musicians, from jazz bassists like Charles Mingus to rock pioneers like Paul McCartney. Lesh's playing was characterized by its melodic sensibility, its rhythmic precision, and its ability to seamlessly blend with the music of his bandmates.

In the early 1960s, Lesh met a group of talented musicians who would go on to form one of the most influential bands in music history: the Grateful Dead. The band's psychedelic sound and improvisational style were a perfect match for Lesh's musical vision. His bass lines provided the foundation for the band's extended jams, anchoring the music and driving it forward.

Lesh's classical training gave him a unique perspective on music. He was able to combine the structure and discipline of classical music with the freedom and improvisation of rock and roll. This fusion of styles made him a truly original bassist, and his influence can still be heard in the music of countless bands today.

Discovering the Bass Guitar

As Lesh delved deeper into the world of rock and roll, he became increasingly fascinated by the role of the bass guitar. He was drawn to the instrument's ability to provide the rhythmic foundation for a band's sound, and he began to experiment with different techniques and styles.

One of the key influences on Lesh's bass playing was the legendary jazz bassist Charles Mingus. Mingus was a master of improvisation and a pioneer of modern jazz, and his music had a profound impact on Lesh's musical development. Mingus's complex compositions and his fearless approach to improvisation inspired Lesh to push the boundaries of his own playing.

In addition to Mingus, Lesh was also influenced by rock pioneers like Paul McCartney and Bill Wyman. McCartney's melodic bass lines and Wyman's steady, driving rhythms helped to shape Lesh's own style. Lesh was particularly impressed by the way that these musicians could create both melodic and rhythmic interest with their bass playing.

As Lesh continued to hone his craft, he began to develop a unique approach to the bass guitar. He was not content to simply provide a rhythmic foundation for the band; he wanted to create something more. He wanted to use the bass to add melodic and harmonic interest to the music, and to push the boundaries of the instrument's capabilities.

Lesh's innovative bass playing would become a hallmark of the Grateful Dead's sound. His deep, resonant tone and his ability to seamlessly weave melodic lines into the band's improvisations helped to define the band's unique musical identity.

CHAPTER 2: THE BIRTH OF THE GRATEFUL DEAD

A Psychedelic Journey

In the mid-1960s, a group of talented musicians came together to form a band that would change the course of music history: the Grateful Dead. At the heart of this groundbreaking ensemble was Phil Lesh, whose innovative bass playing would become the foundation of the band's unique sound.

The band's early years were marked by a spirit of experimentation and improvisation. They drew inspiration from a wide range of musical influences, including folk, blues, jazz, and psychedelic rock. The Grateful Dead's music was characterized by its extended jams, which allowed the band members to explore new musical territories and create spontaneous and unpredictable soundscapes.

Lesh's role in the Grateful Dead was crucial. His deep, resonant bass lines provided the rhythmic backbone of the band's music, anchoring the improvisations and driving the songs forward. His playing was both powerful and subtle, capable of both driving the band's energy and providing moments of quiet introspection.

As the Grateful Dead's popularity grew, so did their reputation for their live performances. The band's concerts were legendary, often lasting for several hours and featuring extended improvisations that could vary wildly from night to night. Lesh's bass playing was a key element of these performances, providing the foundation for the band's sonic explorations.

The Grateful Dead's music was more than just entertainment; it was a spiritual experience. The band's concerts were often described as communal gatherings, where fans could come together to share in the music and connect with one another. Lesh's music helped to create a sense of unity and transcendence, and his bass lines became a symbol of the band's psychedelic ethos.

Shaping the Sound of a Generation

Phil Lesh's unique approach to bass playing was instrumental in shaping the sound of the Grateful Dead. His innovative playing style, characterized by melodic lines, rhythmic drive, and improvisational flair, helped to define the band's distinctive sound.

Lesh's deep, resonant tone provided the foundation for the band's extended jams, anchoring the music and driving it forward. He was a master of creating intricate bass lines that complemented the band's complex harmonies and improvisations. His playing was both powerful and subtle, capable of both driving the band's energy and providing moments of quiet introspection.

One of Lesh's signature techniques was his use of open tunings. By tuning his bass to unconventional tunings, he was able to create a wide range of sounds and textures. This allowed him to explore new sonic territories and to push the boundaries of the instrument's capabilities.

In addition to his technical prowess, Lesh was also a gifted composer and arranger. He contributed to many of the Grateful Dead's most iconic songs, including "Box of Rain," "Eyes of the World," and "Unbroken Chain." His songwriting often reflected his deep spiritual beliefs and his love of nature.

Lesh's influence on the world of music extends far beyond the Grateful Dead. His innovative bass playing has inspired countless musicians, and his legacy continues to live on. He was a true pioneer, a visionary who helped to shape the sound of a generation.

His impact on the music industry is undeniable. His unique style of playing, characterized by its melodic sensibility and rhythmic drive, has influenced countless bassists. His ability to seamlessly blend improvisation with composition has become a hallmark of his work.

Beyond his musical contributions, Lesh was also a beloved figure in the music community. He was known for his kindness, his generosity, and his unwavering commitment to his craft. He was a mentor to many young musicians, and he was always willing to share his knowledge and experience.

CHAPTER 3 : A MUSICAL MAESTRO

The Heartbeat of the Band

Phil Lesh was more than just a bassist; he was the rhythmic heartbeat of the Grateful Dead. His deep, resonant bass lines provided the foundation for the band's extended improvisations, anchoring the music and driving it forward. His playing was characterized by its melodic sensibility, its rhythmic precision, and its ability to seamlessly blend with the music of his bandmates.

Lesh's unique approach to bass playing was a key factor in the Grateful Dead's success. He was not content to simply provide a rhythmic foundation for the band; he wanted to create something more. He wanted to use the bass to add melodic and harmonic interest to the music, and to push the boundaries of the instrument's capabilities.

One of Lesh's signature techniques was his use of open tunings. By tuning his bass to unconventional tunings, he was able to create a wide range of sounds and textures. This allowed him to explore new sonic territories and push the boundaries of the instrument's capabilities.

Beyond his technical prowess, Lesh was also a gifted composer and arranger. He contributed to many of the Grateful Dead's most iconic songs, including "Box of Rain," "Eyes of the World," and "Unbroken Chain." His songwriting often reflected his deep spiritual beliefs and his love of nature.

Lesh's influence on the world of music extends far beyond the Grateful Dead. His innovative bass playing has inspired countless musicians, and his legacy continues to live on. He was a true pioneer, a visionary who helped to shape the sound of a generation.

Innovative Bass Playing and Improvisation

Phil Lesh was not just a bassist; he was a sonic architect, constantly pushing the boundaries of the instrument. His innovative approach to bass playing and improvisation was a key factor in the Grateful Dead's unique sound.

One of Lesh's most distinctive techniques was his use of open tunings. By tuning his bass to unconventional tunings, he was able to create a wide range of sounds and textures. This allowed him to explore new sonic territories and push the boundaries of the instrument's capabilities.

Lesh's improvisational skills were equally impressive. He could seamlessly weave melodic lines into the band's extended jams, creating intricate and captivating bass solos. His ability to improvise in the moment, responding to the other musicians and the energy of the crowd, was a hallmark of his playing.

His deep understanding of music theory and his keen ear for harmony allowed him to create complex and sophisticated bass lines. He was able to move effortlessly between different musical styles, incorporating elements of jazz, blues, rock, and classical music into his playing.

Lesh's innovative bass playing has had a profound impact on the world of music. His influence can be heard in the work of countless bassists, from rock and roll to jazz and beyond. He was a true pioneer, a visionary who helped to shape the sound of a generation.

CHAPTER 4: BEYOND THE GRATEFUL DEAD

Solo Projects and Collaborations

Even after the Grateful Dead's dissolution, Phil Lesh's musical journey continued. He embarked on a series of solo projects and collaborations, demonstrating his enduring creativity and passion for music.

One of his most notable post-Grateful Dead projects was Phil Lesh & Friends. This ever-evolving ensemble featured a rotating cast of talented musicians, including members of other legendary bands like Phish and the Allman Brothers Band. These shows offered a unique opportunity to experience Lesh's music in a new context, with innovative arrangements and improvised jams.

Lesh also ventured into the world of electronic music, collaborating with younger artists and exploring new sonic territories. He was always eager to embrace new technologies and push the boundaries of his musical expression.

In addition to his musical pursuits, Lesh was a dedicated philanthropist. He founded the Terrapin Crossroads, a music venue and restaurant that became a hub for the Bay Area music scene. The venue hosted a variety of musical acts, from emerging artists to established legends, and it quickly became a beloved destination for music fans.

Through his solo projects, collaborations, and philanthropic endeavors, Phil Lesh continued to inspire and influence musicians and fans alike. His legacy as a groundbreaking bassist and a cultural icon endures, and his music will continue to be celebrated for generations to come.

Terrapin Crossroads: A Gathering Place for Music Lovers

Phil Lesh's passion for music extended beyond the stage. In 2011, he opened Terrapin Crossroads, a music venue and restaurant in San Rafael, California. This vibrant hub became a gathering place for musicians, fans, and the local community.

Terrapin Crossroads offered a unique blend of live music, fine dining, and a relaxed atmosphere. The venue hosted a diverse range of musical acts, from emerging artists to established legends. Lesh himself often performed at the venue, leading various bands and collaborating with other musicians.

Beyond the music, Terrapin Crossroads was a place where people could connect and share their love of music. The venue's laid-back atmosphere and friendly staff made it a welcoming space for everyone. Whether you were a die-hard Deadhead or simply someone who appreciated good music and good food, Terrapin Crossroads had something to offer.

Unfortunately, Terrapin Crossroads closed its doors in 2021. However, its legacy lives on. The venue's impact on the Bay Area music scene was significant, and it will be remembered as a place where music lovers could come together and celebrate the power of live music.

CHAPTER 5: LEGACY AND IMPACT

Inspiring Generations of Musicians

Phil Lesh's influence on the world of music is immeasurable. His innovative bass playing, his dedication to improvisation, and his unwavering commitment to his craft have inspired countless musicians. His unique approach to music has left an enduring legacy that continues to shape the sound of rock and roll.

Lesh's ability to blend different musical styles, from jazz to rock to psychedelic, has opened up new possibilities for bassists. His willingness to experiment and take risks has encouraged other musicians to push the boundaries of their own creativity.

Is Enduring Spirit

Phil Lesh was a key figure in the Grateful Dead's extraordinary legacy. His bass playing provided the foundation for the band's iconic sound, and his contributions to their songwriting and improvisational style were essential to their success.

The Grateful Dead's music continues to resonate with fans of all ages. The band's message of peace, love, and understanding remains relevant today, and their music continues to inspire and uplift listeners. Lesh's role in shaping the band's sound and spirit will forever be a part of their legacy.

As we mourn the loss of this legendary musician, we can take solace in the knowledge that his music will live on. His impact on the world of music is undeniable, and his legacy will continue to inspire future generations of musicians and fans.

Conclusion

A Farewell to a True Pioneer. Phil Lesh, the legendary bassist of the Grateful Dead, passed away on October 25, 2024. His death marked the end of an era, but his legacy will live on.

Lesh was a true pioneer, a visionary who helped to shape the sound of a generation. His innovative bass playing, his dedication to improvisation, and his unwavering commitment to his craft have inspired countless musicians.

The Music Lives On. While Phil Lesh may be gone, his music will live on. The Grateful Dead's music continues to resonate with fans of all ages, and Lesh's contributions to the band's sound are undeniable. His legacy as a musician, a songwriter, and a cultural icon will continue to inspire future generations.

As we bid farewell to this legendary figure, let us celebrate his life and his music. May his spirit live on in the hearts of all who love the Grateful Dead.

www.ingramcontent.com/pod-product-compliance
Lightning Source LLC
Chambersburg PA
CBHW070959220526
45471CB00007B/3103